The Mouse's Tale

and other children's sermons

The Mouse's Tale

and other children's sermons

S. Lawrence Johnson

ABINGDON
Nashville

THE MOUSE'S TALE

Copyright © 1978 by S. Lawrence Johnson

Library of Congress Cataloging in Publication Data
JOHNSON, SAMUEL LAWRENCE.
   The mouse's tale.

   1. Children's sermons. I. Title.
BV4315.J637   251'.53   78-858

ISBN 0-687-27255-6

MANUFACTURED BY THE PARTHENON PRESS AT
NASHVILLE, TENNESSEE, UNITED STATES OF AMERICA

To our grandson,
William Lawrence Foulks
and to
Squeaky, the church mouse

CONTENTS

PREFACE

It is difficult to say whether the children's sermon is gaining or regaining popularity. Men like Dr. G. B. F. Hallock collected many fine sermons for children; others such as Patton, Noyes, and Sell wrote excellent books of sermons for youngsters. Today, an ever-increasing number of people, ministers included, are recognizing the value of such sermons and are polishing the art.

The Reverend Kenneth Ensminger, Pastor Ken to his church children, minister of Jerusalem Lutheran Church in Schwenksville, Pennsylvania, has developed the skill to a high degree. Many people are learning it is possible to present a point or get an idea across to adults as well by using the medium of the children's sermon.

Jesus talked about things which people knew in their daily lives. He spoke in parables, short stories that carried a message. He told of the farmer sowing seeds. Some fell on hard ground and died, but some fell on good soil and grew. Everyone knew what Jesus was saying becuse they had experienced these things themselves. The Master told of a girl who had lost a coin from her headdress, then lit a lamp, got down on her knees, and searched until she found that coin. Many of those listening to Jesus had done the same thing. When Jesus reported a mustard seed might grow into a large bush, they all knew to what he alluded. He compared the kingdom of heaven to such a seed.

The best way to impart religious, moral, or ethical values is by using the most elemental terms so they may be understood even by children. Examples picked from everyday events give never-to-be-forgotten lessons. Deep theological thinking is necessary, and philosophers have a profound influence on us. Yet, all the principles they have expounded can easily be illustrated with simple stories.

MR. JOHN CHAPMAN

There have been no motion pictures based on the life of Mr. John Chapman. There has been no television series about him, yet he is one of the best-known men in the history of the western settlement of the United States of America. Have you ever heard his name? Do you know who he was?

The first reliable trace of Mr. Chapman came out of the territory of Ohio in 1801. He had a horse and a little cart loaded with apple seeds. Every once in a while he would hop down from his wagon to plant a few of those seeds. The first orchard this man established was believed to be on the land of a farmer named Isaac Stadden. You may never have heard of Mr. John Chapman, but you do know him well by the name Johnny Appleseed.

At times, Johnny used two canoes lashed together to transport seeds. He would paddle down rivers and streams, stopping all along the way to plant. As soon as his store of seeds became depleted, he would trek back to Pennsylvania for a fresh supply at a cider press. Sometimes he would go into territory where he couldn't take canoes or a horse and wagon, so he would carry the seeds on his back much as a modern backpacker totes a load. He had sturdy leather sacks made because he found canvas ones wore out quickly.

Along with his seeds, Johnny carried his Bible. While he planted the fruit seeds, he also planted seeds of the spirit.

Johnny Appleseed was one of America's first ecologists. He strongly objected to waste of any kind. He thought it sinful to kill any living thing, believing God's soil would provide everything necessary to sustain life. He felt it his particular blessing to be able to converse with God.

For thirty years he wandered, planting apple seeds, planting love, and preaching the gospel through his life and words. Mr. Chapman was a man of strange habits, but he was filled with a great love for all forms of life. Jesus said no person has greater love than the one who would give his life for his friends.

A GREAT FIGHT

In a letter he wrote to his young friend Timothy, the Apostle Paul said, "I have run the great race, I have finished the course, I have kept the faith."

Paul was pleased he had completed what he had set out to accomplish. He was happy he had fought a good fight. He didn't say anything about having won the fight, just that he had finished it. He had run the race of life, done the best he could, and was content.

Larry Quinn usually did a fine job on the track for Shades Valley High School. One day he didn't feel very good, but he knew the coach expected him to run nevertheless. In telling about it, Larry says that just before the race he prayed, "Lord, I don't feel too good. I don't particularly care if I win but I do want to do the best I can. Will you please help me to run the race to the best of my ability?" Larry ran that race. No, he didn't win, but he ran a good race and finished the course.

So often you and I place our emphasis on winning. We can't always win, but we can always do our best.

Do you remember Aesop's story of the tortoise and the hare? The rabbit thought he was special. Racing with a turtle seemed humorous. He could have won the race easily, but he was so sure of himself he lay down and went to sleep. Who won the race? The turtle, of course.

There were none who would say Jesus had won the race when he was killed. But God believed Jesus had run a good race, had fought a good fight.

We don't know who first said it, but this saying is worth remembering: It's not the size of the dog in a fight, but the size of the fight in the dog that counts.

HOW IT CAN HURT

If you were able to wipe away your conscience, you'd be like a balloon without air. What a sorry mess!

The word *conscience* is derived from Latin: *conscrire,* to know. It is not only what *you* know but what *God* knows. Your conscience is always with you. It is like a shadow. You may try to get away from it, but it sticks tighter than glue.

Sometimes we try to make believe we don't have a conscience, or that we've got it so much under control we can keep it from causing us discomfort.

In the first verse of the twenty-eighth chapter of the book of Proverbs it is written, "The wicked flee when no man pursues, but the righteous are as bold as a lion." Adam and Eve had done what the Lord had told them not to do. They were afraid and tried to hide from God. They both had a guilty conscience.

After Cain had killed his brother, Abel, the Lord said, "You shall be a fugitive and a wanderer on the earth." Cain cried out that he would have to hide from God, but he was thinking he would have to hide from his own conscience.

Dr. Hall, a missionary to the Indians in South Dakota, told the story of an Indian who bought a package of tobacco. Later, when he opened it, he found a coin inside the pouch. The Indian took the coin back to the trader. The trader said, "There's no telling how the coin got into the tobacco. It belongs to you."

But the Indian said, "I have a good man inside of me and a bad man. The good man says it isn't mine, to give it back. The bad man says to keep it. When I go to bed at night, the good man and the bad man talk so much I can't get to sleep. I just lie awake. I don't like that."

SMALL POTATOES

Have you heard the story of the farmer in Kentucky who planted his potatoes on the side of a hill behind his cabin so that when he dug them they could roll down into the yard below? He saved himself the effort of carrying them.

There was another man who also planted potatoes. He planted a lot, but not so many that it would have been profitable to have them dug by machine, so he hired two men. Instead of allowing the men to work by themselves, he followed them around, commenting, "Look, you missed these. Sure, they are small potatoes, but they are potatoes, and by leaving them in the ground you are costing me money." Not once did he say, "Thanks, I appreciate the way you fellows are working." It was always complaints and grumbling.

This same farmer never painted his barn, saying, "What's the difference? The cows don't mind." He seemed unable to notice that some of the lap siding was rotting because it hadn't been protected. His machinery was dismal. When he had finished using a tractor or other piece of heavy equipment, he would let it stand corroding in the elements. He would argue, "It runs. Why spend money, time, and effort taking care of it?" There is an old saying this farmer should have considered perhaps: Penny wise, pound foolish.

Jesus must have known people just like this farmer. In the twenty-third chapter of Matthew we find him talking to folks called Pharisees, members of a political-religious party among ancient Jews, who were noted for strict observance of rites and ceremonies. They thought they were pretty good. But Jesus told them, "You give much to the church but overlook things such as law, justice, mercy, and good faith. You are the kind of people who fuss like the dickens when you get a gnat in your mouth, but you'll readily try to swallow a camel. You wash the outside of a cooking pot, but pay no attention to the inside which you leave dirty, filthy. You prepare your food in a dirty kettle and pretend it makes no difference because the outside of the pot shines."

He continued, "Outside you look like honest men, but inside you are dishonest and rotten." Pretty strong words, but you can be sure they deserved them.

It's not just the big things that matter. It's a word of thanks, paint on the barn, a clean frying pan.

THE PLUS SIGN

There is an old country legend about three children, two little boys and a girl. Giovanni, Pietro, and Antonia, Italian children, lived with their parents on a farm. Not far from their home stood a shrine. In many parts of Europe shrines were set up along roadsides so travelers might stop to worship and ask for God's protection on their journey.

These three little children often used to romp around the shrine. They had been taught to respect it as a religious symbol, but it had no particular meaning for them. It had always been there. It was a good place to play.

One day, after they had tired of playing, they lay down in the shade of the cross. The legend relates that the spirit of the Christ came and talked with them, telling stories in a language they understood. The spirit spoke of Jesus' mission on earth. It said, "You are good children. Antonia, you help with the baby. Giovanni, you have an ability to understand numbers, and your father welcomes your help in keeping the family accounts. You, Pietro, are good with the sheep. Your

Father, God, needs your help too. He sent me to teach that he is a God of love who wants his children to do right. God does not force you to be good any more than he forces me to speak to you, but he would appreciate your help."

The legend tells us the children were enthralled by the presence and insisted they wanted tasks to do. They wanted to be God's hands and feet.

Fifty years passed. The shrine remained. Nearby, a beautiful church had been built. Giovanni, who had become a pompous clergyman, returned to preach in it. After the service, the three gathered at the shrine. The spirit appeared and questioned Giovanni, "What have you done with your life?"

"I am in a position of authority in the church. People all over the country know how powerful I am. They have to keep friendly with me if they want to get ahead."

"Have you acted as God's hands and feet?"

"No, I've been too busy."

The spirit turned to Antonia, "How about you? Have you kept your promise?"

"Oh, yes. I have two sons who are priests and a daughter in the convent."

"True. But what have you done to help others?"

"Well, raising a family has taken all my time. Now I'm too old and tired to bother."

When questioned by the spirit, Pietro answered, "I have done little but tend my sheep."

"But, you tended your sheep well, didn't you?"

"I've tried."

"What have you done for others?"

"Little, I'm afraid."

The spirit then talked of those times Pietro had gone out of his way to do many kind things, the love he had spread abroad, the good he had voiced when others had spoken ill, his discounting of gossip.

"Why did you do those things, Pietro?"

"I don't know why, except that each morning as I've prepared to do my daily tasks, I've first looked at this cross, and it has become a plus sign in my life."

Each day, look at the person of Jesus, that his spirit may be a plus sign in your life.

GOD'S GARDEN

Nearly two thousand years ago, the world thought it had buried a man. It had. But it had buried only his body. It thought it would never again hear of him. Later, it realized he was still very much alive. Why? Because his teachings began to bear much fruit. Society had destroyed the body of the man but it hadn't eliminated his thoughts. The man's name was Jesus.

There is little mention of death in the Bible. Death was recognized as a natural thing. It wasn't necessary to talk of it often. Symbols most used in early Christian art were crowns or green palms, emblematic of life. There are very few art expressions of death. This may seem strange for each day people were in danger of torture. It wasn't until the tenth century that folks showed any feelings of gloom or terror about death.

In the spring, your parents may decide to have a vegetable garden. At first, they have to prepare an area for it. They must loosen the soil with a spade or a Rototiller before raking it smooth and dropping seeds carefully into straight rows, then gently covering them with a thin layer of earth. After this come weeks of diligent watering and weeding before the plants become big enough to produce peas, corn, cabbage, tomatoes, which you and your family can eat. Finally, the plants can yield no more. They die. But you still have happy memories of a juicy cantaloupe or a ripe watermelon.

You and I are God's seeds, planted in his garden on earth. At first we were tiny, helpless babies. We began to grow. We're still growing. Oh, some of us are no longer growing physically, but we are, or we should be, growing mentally and spiritually as long as we live on this big blue marble.

We should think of life as God's garden. You and I are eternal. We realize our bodies will wear out someday, but our souls live on forever.

FIRE ANTS

For seventeen years the United States Government was at war, a desperate war, a war in which many suffered frightfully. A large foreign army came ashore at Mobile, Alabama, to invade continental United States. It was fire ants who trekked from Argentina, assailed the coast, and came to give battle.

They first arrived as stowaways aboard a freighter sometime in 1940. In the beginning their spreading was so slow as to be almost unnoticed. Then, like a mighty army, their pace quickened. Now, millions are on the march, stinging as they go. One anthill can house as many as two hundred thousand of these vicious little creatures.

Agricultural scientists thought they were making some headway in their fight for control by using a chemical called Mirex. But they finally realized they were losing. Forces will be regrouped. Other methods of attack will be ventured, but with what results?

It is ironic that it is human contestants in this battle who have been largely responsible for the success of the creatures. In the construction of new office buildings, factories, and homes, bulldozers move large masses of land. For some reason, fire ants spread rapidly in these exposed areas. They also take over pastures that have been overgrazed.

The dreadful sting of the tiny fire ant can be like the sharp thrust of a blunt needle or the touch of a hot match. Those who are particularly sensitive will instantly develop huge red welts or rashes or small white spots and can die if they don't get immediate help. Allergists, doctors who specialize in the treatment of these very sensitive people, instruct their patients to always carry a survival kit containing an inhalent, which they should use as quickly as possible if stung. The poison from the sting can cause a person's larynx to contract, preventing breathing. The inhalent keeps this from happening. The kit may also contain antihistamine tablets to provide temporary relief and a small tube of a soothing ointment.

A nasty remark, ignoring someone, blaming another for your mistakes, all are like the sting of a fire ant.

ACTIONS SPEAK

Do you read a daily paper or a weekly one? Or, do you just read the comics? What advertisements do you look at? Do you seek sensationalism or violence?

There are very few people who get their biographies written up in *Who's Who.* Yet, each of us has a biography that can be read by anyone looking to see. Some folks can tell much about us by the answers we give to such questions as, What comics do you read?

A well-known psychologist says he can tell the type of people living in a house by checking the books and magazines they have in their living room.

Back in the days when *The Saturday Evening Post* was a weekly magazine, a man was asked to write an article for it. Three times he sent in an essay. Three times the editors returned it to him to be rewritten. Now, although this man had considerable literary fame and ability, he couldn't write the story in terms simple enough to be acceptable for this publication. He had fantastic potential. What prevented him from producing an appropriate story?

During holiday periods, thousands of people visit the

beautiful area of nothern Wales. It seems as if there are wall-to-wall trailers, or caravans, as they are called in the United Kingdom. To promote this vacation business, the villagers in one small town decided to announce they would furnish a lifeboat to inspire visitors' confidence in their town. They solicited money and built a house for the boat, but by the time the building was completed they had run out of funds. There still is no lifeboat. Why didn't the townspeople buy the boat first? Lots of words, visions, intentions, promises; some action but not enough.

The ways in which we act indicate much about us to others. As an old adage puts it, Actions speak louder than words.

SODIUM CHLORIDE

When you get into a high school chemistry class, the teacher may tell you to use some sodium chloride. But, you already use it. Almost every day of your life you have used it. You call it salt.

Common salt, or sodium chloride, occurs in the sea, in natural brine in the earth, or in crystalline or rock form. Did you know that there are great masses of salt rock under the city of Detroit, Michigan?

It has been estimated that if the seas dried up they would yield four and a half million cubic miles of rock salt. That would be 14 percent of the entire continent of Europe above the high water mark.

Salt must have been unobtainable to primitive people in many parts of the earth. The *Odyssey,* an ancient Greek story of a man who journeyed the world of his time, speaks of inlanders who didn't know the sea and had never tasted food with salt. There are still sections of Africa where salt is a luxury, and its use is confined to the very wealthy.

Dietitians warn us not to pour away the water in

which we have boiled our vegetables because that water contains natural salts and vitamins. Using this liquid in soups and sauces adds flavor and enhances our health.

Besides being used as a relish or seasoning, salt has the unusual ability to accent the flavor of food. Used in small quantities, it sweetens and freshens the taste of our daily bread.

Also, salt has long been used as a preservative in dairy products such as cheese; in curing fish; in pickling; in preserving hides; and more recently, in refrigeration. Too, it is used in the manufacture of things like chlorine, which purifies our drinking water. It is in bleaching powders and other products we deem essential. It is used in making glass, soap, and enamel. It is valuable in farming, not only in lick-logs for cattle but in the manufacture of insecticides and fertilizers.

Jesus may have eaten something like oatmeal boiled without salt before he said to some of his followers, "You are the salt of the earth, but if the salt has lost its flavor, it might just as well be tossed away because it is no longer any good." What could be worse than salt without flavor?

Jesus recognized it would take a long time to cause many people to follow the way of God but that small groups such as his disciples could have a profound influence. Their attitudes could add savor to many lives.

29

He was aware that such little groups or even one single individual boy or girl could act as preservers of society. If you are a Christian, or would like to be a follower of Christ, you can have a great influence on all the people you meet as you go through life.

WHAT DO YOU REMEMBER?

In his play *Julius Caesar,* writer William Shakespeare said, "The evil that men do lives after them, the good is oft interred with their bones." Isn't it a shame that we must admit the bard was right!

If you will talk with your mother or father they will tell you they like to remember the times when you were good, but these thoughts are overshadowed by the many times you've been a stinker.

The Old West of the United States of America was full of colorful characters. Often you hear people speak of individuals like Davy Crockett, Kit Carson, and others as if they were alive today.

Billy the Kid was one of those characters of the Old West. History remembers him as a bad man, one of the most famous desperadoes of the southwest. If, by magic, you could return to the time when Billy was still alive and visit with some of those who knew him, you would hear stories of Billy's courage, generosity, kindness, and boyish enthusiasm. An old Mexican woman would compare Billy to frijoles seasoned with red chili pepper. She would say, "Yes, he's called a mean man, one with no feeling, but I know better. When no one would help me, Billy was kind to me. Everyone loves that boy. He's so generous."

Jesse James headed an outlaw gang that robbed many trains and midwestern banks. He is recorded in history as a man with nothing but faults. But, according to his brother, Frank, Jesse was tenderhearted, interested in others and their needs rather than his own.

One noon, Jesse and his gang pulled off a main road and stopped at a farmhouse to ask for a meal. After they had eaten, Jesse learned that the woman was a widow and would soon be evicted from her home because she owed fourteen hundred dollars on a mortgage. Jesse took money from his pocket, counted out the bills, handed them to her saying, "Madam this is not a loan. It is a gift."

Are you good? Are you bad? Are you both?

FIRE EQUIPMENT

In Scotland, a little to the north of the half-way point between Edinburgh and Glasgow, lies the ancient city of Stirling. Like Edinburgh, Stirling has a castle standing high above the town, overlooking the countryside. Often during the course of history, this castle has been fought over, and it has changed hands more often than any other place in Scotland.

When you enter Stirling, you go through the portcullis house where a grating of iron hung over the entrance in the great wall. This grating was on chains so it could be lifted up to permit access or dropped to bar access to the castle. As you turn left, you come to a tunnel built in the rock wall. Tunnels such as this were common. It is fun to walk through them, imagining knights of old in clanking armor. From the beginning, this passageway has been known as the Lion's Walk. Hanging on a wall of this walk are long wooden poles, black with the dirt of ages but shiny from use. Fastened to one end of each pole is an iron hook. Even when you learn their name, you still wonder just what is a *fire hook?*

Mary, Queen of Scots, loved Stirling Castle and managed to visit it often. One night, as she lay asleep, a candle flame set fire to the curtains of her bed. She escaped from the room using a fire hook which one of the guards lifted up and caught over her window sill. She used it just as a modern fire fighter would use a fire pole.

For centuries, and still today, roofs of some houses have been covered with straw. This is called a thatched roof. Some roofs of thatch have lasted as long as five hundred years, but usually they last only about three hundred.

One of the disadvantages of such a roof is that it can catch fire. When a fire starts, a fire hook can be used to pull away the burning straw. Thus, fire hooks have had two important roles to play.

At times, all of us are apt to get into trouble of one sort or another. Then we need someone or something to help us. Long ago, the Roman Catholic Church recognized this need and provided what it called the confessional where men, women, boys, and girls might talk about the things they had done wrong or the things they should have done but hadn't. Today, modern counseling services also provide similar opportunities. When you can talk with someone you trust you come to see your life in a better perspective and you feel better. These means of confessing are comparable to fire hooks. They can help pull the fires of temptation and wrong away from you.

SOUVENIRS

A man and his wife made a trip to the Mediterranean. They passed along the north shore of Africa, cruising near Algiers, and on to the city of Ashdod, which was at the height of its importance from 1020 to 587 B.C. and is now one of the two seaports of the state of Israel.

From Ashdod, this couple made a number of trips into the interior of the country. They went *up* to Jerusalem. When you've heard the story of the good Samaritan going *up* to Jerusalem, you probably thought it was just an expression. But the reason for using the word *up* with regard to a journey to that lovely city is because it sits on the top of a mountain, and no matter from which direction you are approaching, you go up.

Another day, the couple took a bus *down* from Jerusalem toward Jericho and along the west shore of the Dead Sea to visit Masada, the site of an ancient fortress built by King Herod the Great as a vacation spot.

Just before this couple had left on their trip, a

neighbor asked them, "Will you please bring me back some stones from the different places you visit?" So, they picked up a bit of rock at Masada. Later, when they walked along the Sea of Galilee at Tiberias, they took a stone from the water to add to the collection.

After leaving Israel, the travelers went to Italy and visited the ancient towns of Herculaneum and Pompeii, south of Naples. In A.D. 79, Mt. Vesuvius erupted, spewing out ash, lava, and a death-dealing gas which killed most of the people in those two cities. Excavation has exposed the areas so folks today can see exactly how people used to live. When they were there, our couple picked up some mortar and a fragment of brick.

When the travelers returned home there was no happier person than their neighbor. One wall of her living room is covered with shelves on which sit hundreds of pieces of stone mementos brought to her from many parts of the world. Perhaps she will never visit the places represented by these bits of rock, but she has read about each city, town, or place, and knows all the facts about them as if she had made a personal trip.

What kinds of souvenirs are you saving from your life? What mementos do you cherish? Do you store up in your heart memories of all the mean things others have done to you, or do you stack up remembrances of kindnesses and helpful deeds?

THE MEASURE OF LIFE

Measurement is one of the earliest skills developed by humans. You use this facility every day. Do you realize how constantly you say, How much is it? How many are there? How tall are you? How wide is it? How many pounds? What time is it?

One of the first things that happened to you after your birth was being weighed and measured by the doctor or nurse. Your mother will tell you exactly the pounds, ounces, and inches you were.

Our clothing is fitted according to our body measurements. Many of the games we enjoy involve measurements. The force of wind is measured daily. We know how much rain falls and what the temperature has been or is going to be the following day.

There are two systems of measure most common in the world today: the old English system and the metric. Early people based their meaurements on units or averages drawn from the lengths of parts of the human body. An early unit known as the cubit was the average length of a man's arm from the elbow to the tip of the middle finger. One of the simplest measures was the hand. This device is still used in determining the height of a horse.

This old English method of measurement is too crude for science, so scientists use the Système International d'Unités, commonly called the metric system. It was first developed in 1799 by French scientists. The unit of length is one ten-millionth part of the distance from the equator to the pole when measured on the meridian. This unit, called a meter, is a little bit more than the English yard.

For centuries we have had good measurements for quality in life. A long time ago, Moses told the children of Israel, "You shall not have unequal weights in your bag, one heavy and the other light. You shall not have unequal measures in your house, one large and the other small. You shall have true and correct weights and true and correct measures."

Our Bible also records a set of measurements that God gave to Moses, the Ten Commandments.

Later, God sent Jesus, who taught us another measurement: to love God and our neighbor as ourselves. It might be well to consider this statement backward: Love yourself, love your neighbor, and you will be bound to love your God.

HOLD ON

Have you ever said, "Hold on, there!" or "Take it easy!"? The apostle Paul wrote to some of his friends, "Stand fast in the Lord." What he was trying to get across was that self-control is very important.

The word *mores* refers to unwritten laws. We know what Congress does, and we say we live by these laws. But equally important are unwritten laws, laws of conduct that have come into being over thousands of years.

There is a story related by a missionary who served in Bengal. Villagers told him a certain path was haunted by demons, that they had actually seen these demons enter a hole in the ground. The missionary felt there must be a logical explanation. He persuaded the villagers to increase the size of the hole. While they were working, out dashed a female wolf. When they dug further, they discovered two very fierce little girls who darted away through the jungle so quickly no one could keep up with them. Finally, they were captured and taken to an orphanage in Midnapore. The children huddled close together, refused to wear clothing, and ate from a dish like cats and dogs. It took years for them to learn to act like normal little girls because in their earliest stages they had had no experience with the *mores* which you have known all your life.

Sometimes we revolt against these mores which would prohibit us from doing certain things we'd really like to do. If we break these unwritten laws, we feel bad even though we may not understand why.

Turn to the person sitting next to you. Hold out your hand. What happens? Most likely your neighbor will hold out a hand to you. It is a natural reaction. A gesture of friendship? Yes, but more. It is a response to an age-old unwritten law about how to be polite.

Discipline is necessary if you are to be happy. Hold on to your tongue—don't say things that might hurt another. Hold on to your heart when an evil person tries to get you to join the gang to which he belongs. Hold on to your feet, guide them in the paths of right. Hold on to the truth. Jesus said, "The truth shall make you free." Finally, hold on to your temper. A quarrel is possible only if more than one person is willing to fight. Hold on!

BEAUTY AND THE BEAST

When it rains in the southeastern part of the United States of America, it is sometimes a soft, warm drizzle, but at other times, it is a deluge. In the past, after farmers had plowed in preparation for planting cotton, rain would often flood down, washing away the soil, carrying off nutriments, leaving only hard red clay.

In 1930 the United States Soil Conservation Service brought from Japan to the south a very beautiful plant named kudzu. This vine has the habit of growing rapidly on poor soil. It was hoped it would quickly send down roots to help prevent erosion and save the valuable elements in the land.

There is no more beautiful sight than a large area covered with kudzu. The leaves are a light green approximately the size of an adult's hand. The vine swiftly spreads over the ground and begins climbing bushes and trees as well. It was learned, however, that kudzu behaves much in the manner of a boa constrictor, twisting itself around and taking the life from its victims, the trees. Beauty and the beast.

At the same time kudzu was being introduced, other

conservation specialists were importing into the south from Brazil a plant called crotalaria. It, too, is a pretty plant. It has striking yellow flowers. It also enriches the soil, adding precious nitrogen, and somehow is able to kill a miserable little bug called a nematode.

Crotalaria was planted in cotton fields and in peach orchards. At first no one worried about the fact that it produces an abundance of poisonous seeds. But later, when one of the major crops of the southeastern area became soybeans, it was a different story. Seeds of the crotalaria are harvested along with the beans. Chickens or cattle eating crotalaria seeds die. The two kinds of seeds can be separated, but it is a costly process. Beauty and the beast.

How often we run into such situations as we are growing up. We meet up with all kinds of things and all sorts of people who seem so very sweet, only to find they can be most harmful. Because of them we can be hurt or others injured.

THE LIGHT OF THE WORLD

William Holman Hunt was born in Cheapside, London, in 1827. Early in life he showed great talent for drawing. He expressed a desire to become an artist, but his father objected. Bill had to work hard and for a long time until he was able to become a painter. Perhaps the best known of his works is a picture called *The Light of the World* painted in 1884. Today it hangs in the chapel of Keble College, Oxford, England. It is a symphony of color.

In the book of Revelation, the writer, John, says, "Behold, I stand at the door and knock, and if any man hears my voice and opens the door, I will enter and have supper with him." Mr. Hunt read those words and caught the dream. Through the wizardry of pigment, he made a pulsing, living tableau of a man standing outside a door that is closed. It seems as if it has never been opened since the day it was set in place. It appears the owner never intended to open it at all. But this pilgrim stands waiting, a stranger at the door of a human heart, hoping it will be opened.

This pilgrim has two crowns on his head. One is a

circlet of gold edged with rays set with jewels. It is the crown of a king. The other is a crown of thorns, a symbol of hate and scorn. If you look closely, you will notice the thorn branch seems to be putting out green leaves of hope.

In his hand, the wanderer carries a lighted lantern suggesting he could light your whole life if you'd let him. Its rays stab into the surrounding darkness. At his feet are red apples to suggest an orchard containing the tree of life, eternal life.

The person in the picture looks strong. He looks strong enough to break down that door if he wanted. But he won't. He'll just keep on knocking until you are ready to open the door.

Harriet Beecher Stowe once wrote:

> Knocking, knocking, ever knocking?
> > Who is there?
> 'Tis a pilgrim, strange and kingly,
> > Never such was seen before;
> Ah, sweet soul, for such a wonder,
> > Undo the door.

JUMPING OVER A WALL

How do you get along with your mom? Are you on friendly terms with your dad? Do you feel you can talk to either one of your parents about things that matter? Are you able to go to them at any time with questions, feeling they will answer you to the best of their ability or tell you where to get the answers you seek?

If you don't feel you can, remember it may not be the fault of your mother or father. It may be that you won't let them talk with you when they feel a great need. It may be they are afraid of you. Does that sound silly? Perhaps it does, but it may be true.

King David had a son named Absalom. Absalom, being the third son, was third in line for the throne. He felt he should be king rather than either of his brothers and gathered around himself agents who prepared an uprising against the father. King David learned of the pending revolt and was faced with one of the most difficult problems of his reign: the capture and punishment of a wayward son. At length, he sent an armed force to overtake this son. In running away from the army, Absalom rode through a thicket, where his long hair got caught in the branches of a tree. As his mule moved out from under him, Absalom was hanged. King David was free of an enemy, but he mourned deeply for his lost son.

In the twenty-second chapter of Second Samuel, we read a beautiful poem of thanks to God in which David sang, "By my God have I jumped over a wall." Walls of ancient cities were thick and high and to get over one called for lots of effort and energy. Constantly, each of us is faced with problems, difficulties which seem too great for us to meet. David met such a problem with regard to his son. He prayed. Then, with God's help and support, he was able to jump over this wall.

Life often seems to be surrounding us with high walls. With God's help we can scale them.

GO CLIMB A TREE

Conscientious doctors have been the same throughout all ages; their primary purpose has been to give relief to those who suffer from illness. Dr. Luke never met Jesus personally, but he became interested in him and made a study of his life. He reported the healing miracles of Jesus very much as he might have written case studies of his patients. In a few words he tells the story of a fellow named Zacchaeus.

Zacchaeus lived in Jericho, a very important trade center at this time. Caravans brought in precious stones, spices, fruits, pottery, balsam, henna, and an aromatic gum valued as a powerful medicine, called the balm of Gilead. From Jericho, these things were distributed into all parts of the then-known world.

Zacchaeus was head of the customs department of the city. This political appointment carried all sorts of opportunities for a person to become a crook. There was no system of checks and balances. It may be this man took every chance that came to him to cheat people. Certainly folks hated and feared him.

When Zacchaeus heard that Jesus was coming

through Jericho, he decided to go and observe him. Now, Zacchaeus was a small man, and it was simply impossible for him to see over the great crowd that had gathered. So he got the idea of climbing a tree. He almost fell out of it when Jesus stopped, looked up, and said, "Hey, come down. I want to stay at your house."

Zacchaeus was a very wealthy man, but he was also a very lonely person. Rumors had been spread about him; folks didn't want to associate with him. He had a bad reputation. He had problems. When he talked over those problems with Jesus he saw himself in a new light. He was able to admit his faults. He realized he really wanted to change, to become a new man and lead a new life.

Because of his job, Zac had been kicked out of the synagogue. This must have hurt him deeply. But, after his meeting with Jesus it didn't seem to matter anymore. He was convinced God had a worthwhile purpose for him. He accepted it. For the first time in his life Zacchaeus felt he was truly Bar Mitzvah, "a child of the commandments."

AT THE POST OF DUTY

Farmers in the United States of America use large combines in harvesting grain. But these wonderful machines are unknown in many parts of the world. The Druse are a political-religious sect of Mohammed origin who live in Israel today. It is fascinating to watch them threshing their grain. First they cut the wheat by hand, then carry it to a flat area where they beat it with a flail, an instrument that looks like a long pole with a shorter one strapped to it so it swings freely. As the grain is beaten, seeds fall to the ground. The straw is picked up and taken away. The remaining seeds and husks are lifted with shovels and thrown into the air. The wind blows away the lighter chaff, while the heavier grain falls to the ground.

We read in the book of Judges that the children of Israel had sown wheat and it was almost ready for harvesting when the Midianites, waging guerrilla warfare took the grain and all the cattle and sheep, leaving the people with no food. For several years the Midianites kept plundering. One year, as a man named Gideon was threshing wheat, an angel appeared and told him to gather an army to go fight the Midianites. When Gideon asked, "Why me?" the angel responded. "Because the Lord wants you to do it and he will help you win!"

Gideon asked for a sign that the Lord really wanted him. There follows an account of how Gideon put a fleece of wool on the ground and said, "I'll believe if tomorrow morning dew is on the wool and not on the earth beside it." Next day the earth was dry but water could be wrung from the wool. Still Gideon wasn't satisfied. He said, "I'll believe if tomorrow the wool is dry and the ground is wet." The next morning the wool was dry and Gideon finally believed.

Then he began the job of assembling an army. At first twenty-two thousand responded. God said this was too many, so Gideon questioned each of them and sent home the eleven thousand who had no interest in fighting. But the Lord said the remaining group was still too many and to take them to a stream and tell them to drink. Those who lay down and lapped the water were dismissed. Only those who knelt and cupped the water with their hands were judged alert enough to be in the army.

It took quite a while for Gideon to make up his mind to do the task assigned to him. He demanded signs before finally putting aside his fear and uttering the same thought later expressed by Jesus, "Thy will be done!"

SLOW DOWN

You can take a jet and go faster than the speed of sound. It will get you where you want to go, and back if you are so minded, in a jiffy.

Most of us live rushed lives. It is like being on a perpetual roller coaster. Young people get so accustomed to this fast pace that if they haven't something to occupy every minute they claim to be bored and ask, "What's there to do?"

Bill Lesher was considered a good pianist by his friends. He went to Europe to study with the great Madame Boulanger. Bill was shocked, almost beyond belief, when he was told it would be necessary for him to practice scales for six months because his technique was sloppy. He'd been getting nowhere fast!

Look at an acorn. It nestles in the earth. The first summer it sends up a little sprout. By the end of the season you can recognize it as a potential tree. But such a tiny tree. It takes years upon years to grow into a mighty oak. The sequoias of California began as tiny little trees. It has taken them hundreds and hundreds of years to become what they are today.

How long did it take to build the pyramids of Egypt? How long was needed to move the great pieces of stone and erect them at Stonehenge in England? The early Romans built a wonderful breakwater at Caesarea on the coast of what is now the state of Israel. This was constructed from huge blocks of stone brought from faraway places. When you look at the remains you are bound to ask, "How could they do it?" The answer is simple: They took their time. They weren't in a hurry.

There is a lovely gospel song that says, "Take time to be holy." Through the psalmist, our heavenly Father said, "Be still, and know that I am God."

STOPPING THE BOAT

Besides being a professionally recognized teacher, the apostle Paul was a tentmaker. His father had been a tentmaker, and it was from him the young man learned the trade. Tents were hand sewn, made from a very heavy cloth that would last quite a long time, until the hot sun caused them to decay or storms ripped them to shreds. Then it was necessary to buy a new tent.

Have you ever moved from one house to another? Or from one town to another? It can be a lot of fun or a miserable experience. It means leaving old friends and places you may love dearly. But it can also be an exciting event for you to meet new people and get acquainted with new areas.

Paul said death was like moving from one tent to another, like disposing of an old one and getting a new one. That is all there is to it.

There is an old Liberian story about Sno-Nysoa, the creator of all things, who sent his four sons to earth. After a while, he wanted them to return home. But they didn't want to leave earth and refused to go back. The father used secret powers to prevent his sons from waking up one morning. He told the people of earth, "I have called my sons home, but I leave their bodies with you."

A famous Roman Emporer named Marcus Aurelius Antoninus once wrote, "Though thou be destined to live three thousand years and as many myriads besides, yet remember that no man loseth other life than that which he now liveth."

A little boy sat on the bank of the Mississippi River. A man came by and said, "You're not fishing, you're just sitting there. Why?"

The boy replied, "I'm waiting for a ship to come."

At that very moment, a boat began to come round the bend, and the boy stood up and began to wave madly.

"Why are you waving like that?"

"Because I want the boat to stop."

"Well, it won't!"

But the boy cried, "Oh yes, it will. The captain is my father."

The boat stopped. The little boy got on. That's what it's like to die. God, our heavenly Father, is captain of the ship. He'll stop it and let us climb on board.

THE GIMMES

Very early in history, people recognized the sun as the ultimate source of life. When gold was discovered in Nubia, south of Egypt, it was thought to be holy because it was the color of the sun. From that time to this, folks have sought gold. Some of the most exciting stories in history are to be found in the chronicles of the search for this metal.

Midas was a mythological king who had a lot of worldly goods but was always wanting more. The god Dionysus granted him his greatest wish: that everything he might touch would turn into gold. Wouldn't that be a wonderful gift, to touch a table and have it turn to gold; to sit on your bed and have it turn to gold; to touch your steak, your french fries, your soda, and have them turn to gold? That's what happened to Midas. He touched furniture; he touched food—they turned to gold. But when he touched his little daughter and she turned to gold, that was too much. He got over his "gimmes" in a hurry.

Centuries ago, people who were the chemists and metallurgists of their age were called alchemists. They were convinced they could produce gold from lead if they could just unlock the secret. They never did, but they were correct in their thinking. Today, we know that if we remove three electrons from lead we have gold.

Hank Porter liked good grades. He wanted good grades, but he didn't want to work for them. Some subjects were easy and he could get A's without any effort. But math was a bore, so each day he copied the work of Dorothy Ostrand who sat next to him in class. Dorothy was fairly good at the subject because she studied it every day, but she wasn't the best. She made mistakes. But Hank didn't know that. One day the math teacher told Hank to remain after class. In no uncertain terms he told Hank exactly what he thought about people who cheated.

Hank got good grades in math—that is, he did until he was caught. He had suffered from a case of the "gimmes."

In industry, a very difficult problem arises when some workers want more money without working for it. They want position but may not put forth the effort required to obtain it. If they are given a responsible job, they may shirk it.

Men, women, boys, and girls all suffer from the "gimmes." Wasn't this what Jesus was talking about when he said to a group of people: "What value is there if a man gains the whole world and loses his soul?"

THE FACE OF GOD

Pass your right hand down over your face, beginning with your forehead. Down the center you feel the bridge of your nose and two eyes on either side. You don't touch your eyes though—your lids are shut. You are aware of hair, your eyebrows and eyelashes. Coming further down, you touch the two holes at the bottom of your nose through which you feel air going in dry and coming out moist. Further down, your hand reaches your mouth. You can open your mouth and put your fingers in or keep it closed.

Now, with your eyes still shut, pretend you are looking in a mirror. You realize you missed something, something you wouldn't want to be without: your ears. They are stiff yet soft. Through them, sound enters and is carried by nerves into your brain.

Sometime, ask your mother or dad to help you with an experiment. Close your eyes and move your hands over their faces. Ask yourself if you would recognize them as your parents just by feeling. Answer honestly.

Dr. Jacob Bronowski wrote a book called *The Ascent of Man.* Right now, you'd find much of it difficult reading, but as you grow older, have it on your list of "musts" for study. He writes about a blind woman who is running her fingers over the face of a man she has never met before. She thinks aloud, "I would say he is elderly. I think he is not English. He has a rounder face than most English people. Probably he is Continental, Eastern Continental. The lines on his face could be lines of agony. At first I thought they were scars. It is not a happy face." She was right. It was the face of a man who had suffered in a concentration camp in Germany in World War II.

Have you ever seen the face of God? Don't laugh. Because, of course, you'll say you haven't. But you have seen interpretations of the face of God. You can comprehend the face of God.

Pick a daisy. Feel the white outer petals, the yellow center. Perhaps you'll get pollen on your finger tips as you examine it carefully. Smell a rose or two or three different varieties of roses. Smell different varieties of orchids. Each has its own fragrance.

From inspecting flowers, trees, animals, insects, or other examples of his handiwork, you can gain a rare understanding of God, for all these things are like his nose, his eyes, his mouth, his ears.

BACK-UP SYSTEMS

Ships that put out to sea must be ready for emergencies. Massive generators in their holds make electricity to light the vessel and to operate its communications systems and the powerful winches that coil what seem to be miles of cables. If one of these fails, there are emergency generators that will go into operation immediately. Should something go wrong with the great steam turbines, diesel engines take over automatically. If, by chance, something should happen to the tiller control mechanism, there are two back-up systems ready, one mechanical, the other manual.

Because of the research of Dr. Jonas Salk and Dr. Albert Sabin, the dread disease of polio is practically unknown tody. But in 1921, Franklin Delano Roosevelt was stricken. His legs became paralyzed, and he was forced to live the rest of his life in a wheelchair. But, there were back-up systems in Mr. Roosevelt's nature. He became a well-known governor and the only person ever to be elected president of the United States for three terms.

Frank Olsen lives in Chicago. For years he's been in a

hospital bed. When he was a small child he began to suffer a crippling form of arthritis. It wasn't long until almost every joint in his body was frozen. Fortunately, he can talk and use his mouth. Frank is brilliant. He instructed a friend how to build a machine that would turn the pages of a book for him. He directed the installation of a series of mirrors whose position he could vary with his tongue. By this means he could look around his room. With determination, be became an electronics specialist. Although he is still confined to a hospital bed, he is consultant to a large electronics firm.

The human brain is marvelous. We have learned that the right side controls the left side of our body; and the left side, the right. It appears that if one fragment is injured, other parts can be trained to take over. If something goes wrong with blood vessels around the heart, others may be developed to take their places.

Who is responsible for the support systems built into each one of us? One of the psalmists said, "Cast your burden on the Lord, and he will sustain you."

THE MOUSE'S TALE

The days immediately following Christmas are almost as hectic for merchants as the few days prior to the event. People bring back all kinds of things to exchange. You may have received clothes that didn't fit and had to be returned to the stores where they had been purchased for substitutions in the correct size. You may even have received duplicate presents that needed to be traded.

However, there are a lot of gifts you have that you can't return. How many times have you thought you'd like to trade your mother or dad for a new one? We sometimes think parents can be problems. You might want to replace them, but you can't—they belong to you.

Remember the day your sister "borrowed" your new dress and spilled soda on it? You were so angry you'd gladly have traded her for Sally's sister. Recall the day your brother was such a stinker? You'd have turned him in for a new model, wouldn't you? But that was impossible. He was a gift you couldn't exchange.

The gifts of God are many. Among them is that of adaptability. Mice conform to all sorts of situations. Because of their adaptability, they have developed into many species, several of which are named for their specially evolved traits. The African climbing mouse has a long slender tail, which he can circle around branches, enabling him to move easily from place to place in trees. His cousin, the pygmy mouse, is so tiny when he is born, he is the size of an adult's thumb nail. Usually he lives in low bushes and tall grasses, but sometimes he can be found nesting in a fallen corncob.

The American pocket field mouse digs tunnels in the earth running eight or ten inches from its home. The Australian field mouse also lives in tunnels. He hides the entrance to his burrow with twigs and shredded vegetation, completely shielding himself. The American spiney mouse looks like a small porcupine.

In Australia, there are ten species of hopping mice. One is called a kangaroo mouse. As you might guess, these small animals look like tiny kangaroos. Another one lives in the desert. He's not only a fast runner but can jump from side to side as well as forward and backward.

Because of the absence of ground cover, mice living in barren areas develop excellent hearing and a wider field of vision than other kinds living in swamps and forests.

These are just some of the many species of mice, each alike, yet each diferent. You've sung, "God is great, God is good." That is true. We should be thankful God has given each of us gifts we are unable to exchange.

WILL BISCUIT EVER LEARN?

Biscuit is a little ball of white fluff called a poodle. She owns a cabin in the White Mountains of New Hampshire. She considers herself kind in permitting the rest of her family to use it with her. She does become incensed, however, over her Pennsylvania cousins, the beagles, when they and their humans visit. Those beagles are big and rough and have no sense of values. They won't stay on the property. They are forever jumping the fence and going for extended romps. They go swimming and then enter the house without drying themselves first. Biscuit's poodle wool dries quickly when she comes out of the water.

Every summer it seems her camp needs painting. It is silly—there is no reason for it—but she supervises the project and ends up with great blotches of paint on her coat. This is annoying. But what is more aggravating is having her mistress trim off the offending wool with huge scissors. In some spots Biscuit is almost naked, but she continues to act as boss.

A main road runs next to Biscuit's cottage. Cars are constantly going to and fro. Hundreds of times Biscuit has been admonished to keep off the road, but invariably, whenever the opportunity presents itself, she goes into the center of the road, parks herself on the yellow line, and basks in the sun, oblivious of everyone. Cars come rushing along. When the driver sees a ball of white, he'll jam on his brakes, stopping the car with a shriek or a squeal just short of the animal. Biscuit sputters and fusses as if to say, "Listen, this is my road. You're on my territory. Stop frightening me." Her master and mistress will race out of the cottage or up from the lakeshore to pluck the poodle out of harm's way and apologize to the people in the car.

After all the times Biscuit has been scolded you'd think she'd learn. The old saying "Experience is the best teacher" doesn't seem to mean much to this little dog.

Do you know any boys or girls who are like Biscuit? Do you know any boys or girls who, regardless of how often they are hurt, regardless of how often they do harm to others, never learn?

NOTE: Biscuit's learning experiences have been recorded in The Pig's Brother, The Squirrel's Bank Account, *and* Captain Ducky, *but there will be no more stories about her. Little Biscuit was run over by an automobile. She never learned. She died shortly after this story was written.*

WASTE NOT, WANT NOT!

For a number of years, Mrs. Stewart, now of Detroit, Michigan, was soup chef in Buckingham Palace for King Edward VI. For her use in the kitchen there were large copper kettles about the size and somewhat the shape of modern garbage pails.

These vessels shone like burnished gold from constant polishing. Parings from vegetables were carefully scrubbed and tossed into one of these pots. Scraps of meat, bones left over after the carving, all were added to the huge kettle. Then it was covered with water and put on to simmer for hours.

After it was all well cooked, the liquid would be drained from the spigot at the bottom of the kettle and strained through cheesecloth. The bits of food left in the pot were emptied onto compost heaps and later dug into the gardens to help produce more vegetables with which to make more soups. Mrs. Stewart delights in telling about the king's love for consomme. She comments, "Nothing that came into the king's kitchen was wasted, not one single thing. His Majesty couldn't afford to be wasteful."

Quite a different philosophy is shown by ocean-going freighters carrying lubricating oil in sixty-gallon steel drums. These drums are quite expensive so you would expect that, when emptied. they would be taken back to home port for re-use. But that isn't the case! Oil companies won't buy them to be used again. So, when sailors have drained a drum, they knock holes in the tops and bottoms and cast them overboard where they sink to the bottom of the ocean.

Debbie and Chris went to a potluck supper at the church. Everything looked delicious. The two loaded their plates with food. Debbie and Chris ate some of the food, but most of what they had so generously served themselves they left on their plates. A lot of good food had to be dumped into the garbage pail.

There's an old adage worth remembering: Waste not, want not!

WHAT A CHARACTER

Joseph C. Lincoln, a Massachusetts author, wrote *Cape Cod Ballads* and several other excellent books. Mr. Lincoln had met interesting and fascinating people and drew some marvelous pen portraits of them. It was he who asked, "What is a character?" He responded to his own question, "Why, he or she is apparently an individual who speaks and acts in a manner different from that in which you yourself speak and act and think. And it's just possible that he, because of that difference, may consider you a character."

John Hancock, son of the minister of the Congregational Church in Braintree, Massachusetts, was the wealthiest New Englander on the patriot side in the Revolutionary War. You remember him as one of the signers of the Declaration of Independence. He wrote his name in very large letters. In referring to a signature placed on a document, folks began to speak of it as one's "John Hancock." "Put your John Hancock here!" became an accepted and understood expression.

Tradition has it that Mr. Hancock said, "I made my

signature bold so that John Bull can read it without his glasses." What a character!

John the Baptizer was a scrawny man who possessed a loud voice. He came out of the wilderness crying to people to remember the difference between right and wrong. He told them to stop doing what was bad and to turn around and do what was good. He shouted, "Repent!" He openly accused King Herod of doing wrong. Because of this, he was beheaded. What a character!

Jesus told us we should love one another. He said we should love our enemies, not hate them. He taught that if someone hits you on one cheek you should turn around and let them hit the other cheek too. He said if someone wants us to walk one mile with him we should be willing to walk seven. He taught a lot of other "crazy" things. What a character!

AN APPLE CORE

Have you ever watched your mother preparing apples to be baked for dessert? She picks up a lovely McIntosh, takes an apple corer to carefully remove the entire center, stuffs the hole with raisins, sugar, nuts, and maybe even a few miniature marshmallows.

When your father wants an apple to eat, he chooses a shapely Jonathan, quarters it with his pocketknife, cuts out and tosses away the core, and proceeds to enjoy his snack.

You prefer a Red Delicious apple that has been kept in the refrigerator so that it is cold. It's crisp and juicy and fills your mouth with a sweet yet tart liquid. You hold the apple between your thumb and forefinger, one placed at either end. You carefully eat around the core, which you toss away when you're finished.

What about an apple core—isn't it any good at all? If you believe it isn't, you're mistaken. Actually, it would probably do you good to eat the core. It has two major parts: the stiff, bark-like membrane and the seeds. Both the coarse substance and the seeds would add roughage to your diet.

Dyslexia is a disturbance in the brain that causes some people to have a difficult time reading and spelling. Sometimes, a person so afflicted will see the letters of writing or printing upside down or in reversed order. It may be hard for folks with this malady to express themselves. They'll say, "You know I can't read. How do you expect me to get my lessons? I can't!"

Wait a minute. Consider some people who have had this condition. What would our modern world be had it not had Thomas Edison? His list of inventions seems endless. Woodrow Wilson was unable to learn the alphabet until he was nine. He couldn't read until he was eleven. He grew up to be not only a college professor but a president of the United States of America. Hans Christian Andersen was a great author. Dr. Albert Einstein was a renowned scientist.

Nelson Rockefeller was graduated from Dartmouth College with honors, became governor of the state of New York, and served as vice-president of the U.S.A. Like so many others, he could easily have said, "I can't," and let things go. He was another person with dyslexia who realized that underneath he had potential but would have to work harder than his peers.

Everyone cannot reach the stature of greatness, but within each one of us is a core of wondrous abilities.

TOUCH OF A HAND

When Tommy was a baby, his parents took him to wish bon voyage to a family friend about to sail to England. It was a lovely day. The trip to the docks in Boston was a lot of fun for the family. Before he said good-bye, the man wanted to hold the little boy. When the friend touched him, Tommy screamed as if he'd been burned with a hot iron. What was it in the touch of this person that so distressed the baby?

A young man strained his heart and suffered a great deal of pain. Medical doctors were unable to find anything to ease his discomfort. One day an elderly clergyman stopped in for a visit and asked where the pain seemed to be the most severe. Then he placed his fingers on the sick man's chest just over his heart and very slowly moved them toward the left shoulder and down the left arm. In telling about this experience, the young man stated that the pain appeared to be following the older gentleman's fingers untl it left his body. What happened? No one knows, but sometimes there seems to be magic either good or bad, in the touch of another human being.

In ancient days, the "laying on of hands" was considered a means of giving blessing. Today, if you attend the ordination of a minister, you will see all the clergy at the ceremony gathering round to place their hands on the head of the candidate. This is regarded as a means of passing on a sacred trust and tradition. Some candidates have reported they have felt a "power" enter their bodies when the hands were on their head.

The late Kathryn Kuhlman was a well-known faith healer. When people who were ill came before her, she would touch them on the forehead. Almost immediately, they would start to fall to the ground and one of Miss Kuhlman's assistants would have to catch them. No one could explain what had taken place, but a person with faith would be cured.

Leprosy was the most dreaded of all diseases at the time Jesus was alive. Today, we know leprosy is caused by bacteria, but we still find it difficult to keep under control. Once as Jesus was leaving a hillside where he had been speaking, a crowd followed him. A man with this horrible disease approched the Master. Ordinarily, a leper was required to cry aloud, "unclean, unclean," as a warning to folks to keep away, for people believed if you touched such a person you would die. This man called to Jesus, "Sir, if you will, you can make me clean!" Jesus reached out his hand and touched the man and he was healed.

C. S. Biggs wrote:

> Hold Thou my hand, dear Lord,
> Hold Thou my hand;
> I do not ask to see, or understand;
> Only that Thou wilt be
> Constantly near to me,
> Holding my hand, dear Lord,
> Holding my hand.

GLUE IT

From earliest times, people have used glue. Over three thousand years ago Egyptian craftsmen had learned the art of veneering. They boiled animal bones and skins until they became a sticky mass that would adhere to different substances. They also developed methods of gluing reeds together to make papyrus, a kind of paper. Today, scientists have discovered how to use modern adhesives to bind fibers so as to create many new kinds of paper, cloth, or material similar to cloth.

When your great-grandmother wanted to seal together two sheets of paper, she used the white of an egg as glue or a paste made from flour and water.

Various sorts of adhesives have either been discovered or developed during the last few years. *Epoxy* is a familiar world. But some of the names sound strange. Have you heard of *neoprene, ethylene, acrylics, ureaformaldehyde, polyvinyl acetate, polyvinyl alcohol,* or *cyanocacrylate?*

Glue is much lighter and stronger than rivets so it is used in putting airships together. Sometimes more than a half ton of glue is used in one plane. All helicopter blades are bonded with adhesives. Many modern automobiles contain as much as twenty-five pounds of glue.

Undoubtedly you have heard advertised a glue that takes only three drops to bond metal to metal so strongly that an auto may be lifted from the ground without the glue letting loose.

One of the most powerful adhesives in the world is called by a four-letter word—*love.* If used properly, it can be the most wonderful product available to humans. A psalmist once wrote, "They shall prosper that love Thee." Through the application of love, nations might be bound together. All your lives you have been hearing or reading about war. There have been many civil wars, wars between people of the same nation. Differing factions might have been bound, one to the other, with the application of a little love.

This effective cement of *love* can withstand a lot of abuse. The writer of the Song of Solomon recognized this fact, singing, "Many waters cannot quench love, neither can floods drown it."

Rabbi Julius Gordon once affirmed, "Love is not blind; it sees more, not less. But because it sees more it is willing to see less." Think about that.

Do you know any situations or circumstances where love might help?

RECORDS

Young men and women going into the ministry study at a theological school after they have been graduated from a college or a university. Many of these theological schools require each student to put in a year of internship as a part of his or her training.

The student may go into an established parish to work under the direction of a senior minister, learning some of those skills that can be acquired only in an on-the-job situation, or an intern may be sent by a denomination into a deprived area, rural or inner city. Experience in any church or location can be exciting, productive, and hard work.

Before the year of internship was introduced, some church groups provided their students opportunities to do what was termed student summer service.

The young person would receive room, board, transportation, and a small amount of money. The individual would work very hard during the summer months in a parish, teaching Vacation Bible School, working with young people, becoming involved in community affairs, or doing whatever was necessary in the locality. One of the most important gains was learning to serve the hale and hearty as well as those who were ill or in great trouble.

Dr. Robert Schuller, minister of a large church in Garden Grove, California, tells a rather frightening story but one that carried a message for him and for us.

He was serving for a summer as pastor on an Indian Reservation. One evening, as he was returning to his quarters, he was stopped on the street by a man waving a large knife. Over and over he kept saying he was an angel sent by God to "destroy the records." Dr. Schuller reports he was frightened but talked quietly and invited him to his room. They talked a long time. Finally, the stranger announced he was tired, so Dr. Schuller fixed a bed on the couch for him to sleep.

The next day, he learned the man had escaped from a mental hospital and was considered dangerous. Dr. Schuller assures us that there was a very real message in this experience.

He contends that each of us holds many records in our library of thoughts that we ought to destroy. Some of these thoughts are about things we have done that we should not have done, and the memory of them brings pain. These we should destroy. Others that should be destroyed are remembrances of meanness people have inflicted upon us. It is never healthy to hold in our hearts such records. They need to be destroyed.

There are other records, though, that should be kept fresh. The writer of the book of Deuteronomy was fearful lest the Children of Israel should erase the record of the goodness of God toward them. He wrote, "Remember all of the way which the Lord thy God led thee." It is easy to keep a record. The problem we have is in keeping a record correct.

THE CLEAT

A young couple with three young sons bought an old farm on the outskirts of a small town northeast of Philadelphia. The stone farmhouse, its outside walls covered with stucco, is one hundred fifty years old. The walls are sixteen inches thick. Downstairs, there is a large room across the front and a huge kitchen at the back. Upstairs there is one big room, three small ones, and a bath. This bath is a fairly recent addition, installed about 1920.

Being young and ambitious, the father and mother undertook the renovation of the property themselves. For about fifty years nothing had been done in the way of maintenance except adding one layer of wallpaper over another. All this paper had to be peeled to get down to the bare plaster underneath. Outside, the five acres had become a veritable jungle. But for the parents, clearing was fun.

On the floor upstairs, right in the traffic pattern between two of the rooms and the bath, is a wooden cleat, a piece of wood jutting up from the floor. The floorboards are of wide pine, but the cleat is oak. The couple couldn't understand the reason for this strip of oak. The father wanted to pull it up and throw it away until the mother pointed out that it had been fastened with old square-cut nails, indicating it had been there many years.

One day, the former owner, a lady who had lived in the place for over fifty years, stopped by to see what they were doing with "her house." The family asked about this wooden strip. She looked at them in amazement, "Why, land's sake, that's how you get into the attic." At first this explanation was as puzzling as the bit of wood itself. Then they realized it must have been fastened there to keep a ladder to the attic from slipping. Without this strip it would be impossible for one person to mount a ladder alone. Someone would have had to hold the bottom to keep it steady. Even though they didn't plan to use the attic, they decided to preserve the cleat anyway. Now the cleat, a real part of history, is a conversation piece.

The Old Testament tells us the story of Moses, how he went to the top of a mountain and there had a conversation with God. God showed him the Land of Promise and talked about the behavior of the Children of Israel. Then God gave Moses a set of specific laws. The Lord said if the Children of Israel would accept these laws they would have a firm foundation on which to develop, and would become a worthwhile and progressive people. You may read these laws in the twentieth chapter of Exodus. Even today they can act as that old cleat did, anchoring us in place. In church school you are told that Jesus taught this or Jesus suggested that. Often, it is hard to try to follow his teachings. It's difficult to be honest. It's impossible to bear someone else's burden. It's impractical to forgive people when they wrong us. It's ridiculous to love our enemies. It's absurd to love the people we know don't like us. These suggestions of Jesus' can be annoying. They can be inconvenient. But, they also can give the firm foundations we need.

EVERLASTING LIGHT

It is hard for city folks to imagine a town without streetlights. But they are a comparatively recent addition to our way of living.

In 1417, the Lord Mayor of London ordered all house owners to hang a lighted lantern over their front doorway at night. Not until three hundred years later did the City of London take over responsibility of providing streetlights.

Time came when, at dusk each evening, lamplighters would walk along streets turning on these lights. Since the lights were set on tall pedestals, each man carried a seven-foot pole that had a flame at one end. Also, it had a notch that would fit around a handle on the lamp which would turn on a valve, letting gas flow.

At one time there were sixty thousand gas streetlights in London. But, with the development of the electric arc light, gaslights began to go out of style.

Generally, we credit Thomas Edison with the discovery of the incandescent light. However, almost immediately after the development of the electric battery, people became aware that an electric current passing through a wire gave off both heat and light according to the resistance of that wire. In 1859, a man named Moses Farmer, who lived in Salem, Massachusetts, lighted his home with electric lamps which used platinum wire as the light-giving element.

Edison was certain he could develop a filament that would be cheaper and more effective than platinum wire. He experimented with thousands of materials, even trying human hair. He concluded carbon was the most satisfactory.

The search for better, more efficient light has produced many types. After the carbon lamp came the tungsten filament. The quartz tubular lamp is about two inches long. This may seem small, but there are some lamps in use that are much smaller, even tinier than a grain of rice.

Fluorescent lights use less energy than tungsten incandescent lights and are used in many homes, schools, and offices. You probably have seen sodium vapor lights, a brilliant yellow, that penetrate fogged-in areas and are used to light highways. And, at airfields, you have noticed lamps filled with krypton which give off bright flashes of light.

Various types of light illuminate situations. God has used different happenings as lights to illuminate directions we should take. God wanted Jonah to go to the city of Ninevah. Jonah didn't want to go. God had to use harsh light to illuminate the way for him. God caused a whale to swallow then cough up Jonah on the shore near Ninevah. Jonah still ignored the message. God destroyed a tree that was shading Jonah from the glare of the sun. The heat became so intense that the poor old fellow thought he'd be burned to ashes. Jonah finally responded to God's light.

FRANKINCENSE AND MYRRH

In the Christmas story we read about scholars who came out of the East, wise men we call them, who brought gifts to the infant Jesus of gold, frankincense, and myrrh. You know what gold is, but what about the other two?

If you tap a maple tree you get a sap that can be boiled into a delicious syrup. If you tap various tropical trees you get an elastic substance we call rubber. If you tap certain East African trees you obtain a gum resin called frankincense. For centuries people burned frankincense for the sweet smell of the smoke. It was used in services of worship for it was believed the fragrant vapors would carry the prayers of the congregation into the nostrils of God. It was a valuable substance.

Myrrh comes from a tree that grows low to the ground, almost a bush. It exudes a soft yellowish gum from its stems and branches. Later this gum turns oily and drops to the ground. It was used as a holy anointing oil.

There is a legend about a girl who lived in a land that was usually lovely and green, but a drought had dried up the lakes and streams. All the people were thirsty. This little girl's mother was very ill and needed water, so the girl traveled far from home in search of some. She sought until she was exhausted. She prayed for enough rain to fall to fill her cup with water. She fell asleep. When she awakend, the cup was full. She started home. On her way she saw a little dog, panting. She stopped and put a few drops of the precious water into the animal's mouth. The cup turned to silver. She began to run. When she arrived home her mother refused to drink, insisting she was dying and didn't need the water. She told her daughter to take the water to others. The cup turned to gold.

As the child left the hut, a stranger appeared. He was so thirsty his tongue was cracked and swollen. The child offered him some water and the cup became encrusted with diamonds. The stranger said, "Blessed are those who give a cup of water in my name." As he finished speaking, the cup seemed to be lifted from his hands into the heavens. If you look into the sky at night you may see that cup. Folks call it the Big Dipper.

Each of us has gifts to give. They may not be gold, frankincense, or myrrh, but we can give cups of cool water. Jesus said, "It is more blessed to *give* than to receive."

A MATTER OF FAITH

In olden times, stone masons and tentmakers wore aprons similar to those used today by some carpenters. The apostle Paul, a tentmaker, had the reputation of being a magician. It was thought he had great powers and those powers were transferred to whatever had come close to him. People said if you touched one of Paul's aprons marvelous things might happen to you, if you had faith.

There was a busy little port on the Sea of Galilee called Capernaum. In the day of Jesus it was called Kapher-Nahum, meaning town of Nahum. Jesus used this village as the center of his Galilean ministry. There's a great story in Matthew's gospel about something that happened in this town.

Rome ruled this area and had soldiers stationed here to keep order. An officer in charge of one hundred men was called a centurion. One centurion, who had never met Jesus but knew his reputation, particularly his miracles of healing, approached the rabbi and said, "Sir, I have a servant who is completely paralyzed and in great pain." Immediately Jesus responded, "I'll come right now and see him."

"No, you don't need to come, that won't be necessary. Just say the word and I know my servant will be healed."

The Master turned to those standing nearby and remarked, "I tell you, nowhere have I seen such faith." Facing the man, he said, "Go home. Because of your faith, your servant will be well."

Seafaring men are acquainted with strange pale flames that seem to come from mastheads or the ends of spars on their vessels. No one knows exactly what they are, but they are called St. Elmo's fire.

Captain Bob Larsen used to tell about his experience with St. Elmo's fire. It was in a gale. "We saw lights dancing on the bowsprit of a French ship which had been badly battered. I yelled that she was on fire, but one of the others said I was wrong, it was St. Elmo's fire. He declared that St. Elmo, the sailor's patron saint, would see the men on board safely through the gale.

"That night the storm grew stronger. I was sure the French ship and our own would never get to shore. But when the storm subsided the next day, we sighted the French ship and went to help her before she could fill with water and sink. We took off the eighteen crewmen and got them into Gloucester. Some of them were badly hurt, but all of them lived. It was a miracle. They believed St. Elmo would save them, and he did."

John records that, after the Resurrection, when Thomas was skeptical, Jesus said to his disciples, "Because you have seen me you have found faith. Blessed are those who have never seen me and yet have found faith."

A MYSTERY

Ebenezer Litchfield tumbled from his bed, hurried into his clothing, and quickly made his way down the ladder into the kitchen of his home in the community of Wakefield, New Hampshire. Ordinarily, Ebenezer would have gone right out to the barn to help his father milk the three cows, but this day was different for he was to take a load of wood to farmer Wentworth over by Ivanhoe Pond.

Ebenezer ate his breakfast and trudged out to the wagon which he and his father had loaded the previous day. He gave a "giddap" and the team left the Litchfield yard and started along Ballard's Road. Level ground was easy, but the drag up hills was a strain. On one long hill the boy stopped the oxen for a rest at a thank-you-ma'am—a hump, like a modern speed breaker, which was built into the road to hold a wagon from rolling backward.

It is doubtful if those who built this thank-you-ma'am ever thought Ebenezer would one day use it with appreciation. Nor did Ebenezer realize that a hundred years later lots of people from many parts of the United

91

States of America would travel over this same thank-you-ma'am in gas-driven buggies called automobiles, concerned over something strange which had happened nearby.

On the tenth of January, 1977, Mr. and Mrs. William McCarthy were in their house not far from the thank-you-ma'am when Bill glanced out at the blizzard and noticed a hole in the pond. He went outside to study it. The ice seemed to have melted from the top and bottom at the same time. He went back in to phone the Wakefield police. Shortly after this he noticed his digital watch had stopped.

The police brought in a Geiger counter and found an exceptionally high amount of radiation. The following day, state officials took further readings, declared the radiation within normal limits, but told the McCarthys to keep folks away from the pond.

The happening was broadcast to the nation. Many came to look. What had caused the hole? Was it, as some people thought, an unarmed missile that had fallen from a B-52 flying a training mission from Pease Air Force Base? Various scientists and government representatives gathered information, but if they learned anything, it has never been reported. The theory accepted by most folks living in the area is that a bit of space junk tumbled down from heaven.

One of the most difficult things we modern humans have to do is admit there are things we don't understand. We keep sending space ships into the heavens to try to explore other planets. We develop more and more powerful microscopes in order to learn more about the infinitesimal in our universe.

As quickly as we learn one fact about this world God has created, there appear more pieces of information demanding study and possible understanding. It was Paul who told the people of Corinth, "The Spirit searches all things, all the deep things of God."

LOYALTY

Sometimes in church we use a hymn that says:

> He who would valiant be
> 'Gainst all disaster,
> Let him in constancy
> Follow the Master.

The Duke of Wellington was one of England's great soldiers. During his lifetime he was often referred to as the most influential person in Europe. Customarily, the very wealthy and the titled had little respect for the rights of those whom they considered to be beneath them. When they would go on a fox hunt, they would thoughtlessly ride across the gardens and fields of local farmers. One day, a farmer closed the gate to a field of wheat, set his son on guard, and told him that under no circumstances was he to open it. Later, mounted men came charging up and demanded the gate be opened so they could pass through. The youngster refused. One of the men cried, "Boy, I don't think you know who I am. I am the Duke of Wellington."

The farmer's son responded, "Yes, my lord. You expect loyalty and obedience from your men. My father expects it from me. He told me not to open the gate to anyone."

The duke smiled and the group rode off.

Skye Terriers have short straight legs, long low bodies, and long heads. These dogs from the Isle of Skye are known for their love and loyalty.

A poor shepherd living in Scotland had one of these terriers named Bobby. When the shepherd died, they buried his body in Greyfriars Churchyard off the Royal Mile not too far from Edinburgh Castle. Bobby followed his master's casket to the cemetery, lay down, and refused to leave. There were many who would have been happy to adopt the little dog, but Bobby wouldn't move from the grave. Kind people brought him food and water.

The Lord Provost of the city gave Bobby a collar and issued him a permanent license. For fourteen years, in rain, in snow, in fog, in clear weather, Bobby stayed by his master.

After Bobby died, the Baroness Burdett-Coutts commissioned a statue of Bobby which was placed near the main gate of the cemetery. To this day, Greyfriars Bobby continues his vigil.

Constancy, loyalty, devotion, no matter what you call it, it's a trait of character to be desired.

I LOVE YOU

There is a legend that when Saint Peter was a very old man, his sight and hearing almost gone and unable to walk, he would be carried through the streets to worship in the church. He would lift his hands in blessing saying, "Little children, love each other." So began the traditional blessing of the people by the pope.

Jesus had much to say about love. It is recorded in the Gospel of John that on one occasion he said, "By this all men will know that you are my disciples, if you have love for one another." It was reported by Matthew that Jesus asked the question, "If you love those who love you, what reward have you?" There may be a great deal of reward.

When did you last tell your mother or your dad you loved them? You think it's silly to tell your parents you love them? It's not. They'd appreciate hearing the words.

The art of making clocks is a very old one. Next to the famous Sheldonian Theater in Oxford, England, is a museum that houses a wonderful collection of ancient timepieces. One day in 1583 Galileo, sitting quietly in the cathedral in Pisa, Italy, became aware that a lamp hanging on the end of a chain was swinging back and forth. He thought this same swinging principle might be used in the construction of a clock. Both he and his son, Vincent, tried but failed to construct such an instrument. The first successful clock using a pendulum was made by a Dutch scientist, Christian Huygens.

A pendulum consists of a length of wire, rope, or string from which a weight is suspended. Moving the weight up the wire speeds up the swing of the pendulum and moving it down the wire slows it. The time taken for the swing depends on the pull of gravity. Without the weight, or the bob, the supporting string or rod hangs lax.

Boys and girls all have the same problem of regulating themselves in their relations with others. The weight, bob, or compensating element is love.

There are many grand stories about Dr. David Livingstone but none more touching than of the time he was invited to speak to students at Glasgow University in Scotland. He said, "Shall I tell you what sustained me in my exiled life among strangers whose language I couldn't understand? It was this that comforted me at all times: 'Lo, I am with you always, even unto the end of the world.'" Dr. Livingstone felt sure in his heart he was loved by the spirit of God through Christ so he could withstand any hardship.

Out of the highlands of Scotland came a story that

has been told and retold. You may have heard it before. A little girl was carrying a little boy as best she could. It was evident she was staggering under her load. A man seeing the children said, "How heavy your task must be!"

The young girl replied, "He's no heavy. He's me brither!" But the story doesn't say she told her little brother she loved him. Certainly she showed love. You have heard, Actions speak louder than words. But words are music to the ears.

Getting along in life is easier if you will remember to say three little words: I love you!

IN THE BACKGROUND
OF EASTER

Have you heard the song "The Easter Parade"?
The practice of parading around showing off new
clothing after church services on Easter dates back to a
very old custom of newly baptized members of the
church wearing white robes. As they marched around,
they could be easily recognized as new fellow Christians
and were given a warm welcome by long-standing
members.

Eggs symbolize new birth, so you can figure out why
they have been involved in traditions of Easter. You
probably think only of coloring eggs and having egg
hunts, but according to records found in Chester
Cathedral, England, it used to be that clergy and choir
played a kind of ball game with eggs on Easter Sunday
morning. The bishop would carry eggs into the church.
At one point in the service everyone would begin to pelt
those eggs at one another. Afterward, they would have
a communal breakfast of gammon (ham) and tansy
pudding (a sort of omelet flavored with the juice of
tansy, a bitter herb signifying immortality).

Greek children used to color eggs red for the blood of Jesus, green for home, and blue for health. They carried the red eggs to church on Easter Sunday. After the church service, they would have an egg-cracking contest, symbolic of the breaking of the seal on the tomb of Jesus. As the eggs were broken, they would cry, "Christ is risen!"

Early church leaders incorporated many pagan customs into the celebration of Easter. One interesting habit still found in some parts of Europe has to do with the "corn mother." People used to believe spirits inhabited everything. The finest ears of grain were separated and kept until spring, then planted. It was thought this corn mother contained the spirit of the grain and when it was planted the spirit would be released so the crop would be plentiful.

In Sicily, that little football-shaped piece of land at the toe of Italy, seed corn was hidden in the dark until Good Friday, then planted on the graves of loved ones. As the seed matured, friends were reminded of the new life Jesus had promised. Perhaps the belief of some folks in the southern states of the United States that the best time to plant a garden is on Good Friday stems from this ancient practice.

In times long past there was worship of a god called Adonis, ruler of spring and summer. Growing grain and wax figures were used in worship of him. The Roman Catholic Church in some parts of the world took over some of this procedure. They place a wax image in a coffin and cover it with lemons, roses and other flowers. On the evening before Easter, priests carry this coffin through the streets while other priests swing incense pots in the belief that the odors will drive away evil spirits.

Gypsies have a ritual in which they take herbs and bits of dried snake and lizard and place them in a wooden box. Each member of the tribe touches these items. They gather on the bank of a river or stream, throw burning brands into the water, and finally the wooden box. It is their conviction that this box contains all the evil thoughts of each person and each can now start a new year with a clean heart.

Tradition tells us that the decision as to where the disciple James was to be buried was left to chance. Oxen were hitched to a cart. His coffin was placed in the cart and the animals whipped off. Where the oxen stopped they buried the body of James. That spot is in the town of Santiago in Spain, and a lovely cathedral marks the site. On the night before Easter, thousands gather in front of this cathedral for a festival. As the clock strikes midnight, each person begins to eat grapes, and together they repeat the words Jesus said unto his disciples at the Last Supper, "This do in remembrance of me!"

TRIBUTARIES

The Latin word *tributarius* originally meant paying a tribute, a tax or fee, for protection but eventually came to be applied to streams, brooks, runs, or branches that gave their water into a river.

In the United States of America, the great Mississippi begins with a stream flowing from a small lake in the northern section of Minnesota called Lake De Soto. From there it moves languidly a few short miles until it empties into Lake Itasca. Here it stands, or seems to stand quietly, as if resting in preparation for its long and tumultuous journey to the Gulf of Mexico.

The Red River of the North, flowing along the western border of Minnesota, runs into Lake Traverse. It continues through Big Stone Lake and becomes the Minnesota River, which pours into the Mississippi at Minneapolis. Along the banks of all great rivers towns have been built which have grown into sprawling cities.

The Jordan River has its beginning in the Huleh swamps from which it empties into the lake we call the Sea of Galilee. Perhaps a better name for this lake would be what many in its vicinity call it: *Chinnereth,* meaning "harp." If you look carefully at a map of Israel you will realize how much the shape of the lake resembles a harp. The lake is about two hundred feet deep and lies nearly seven hundred feet below sea level. It is forty-six miles long and its greatest width is nine and a half miles. During the time of Jesus there were many towns on the shore of this lake. The whole area was a great center of commerce and learning. Jesus was a carpenter. His father was a carpenter. Carpenters were the prosperous members of society, as were the fishermen. Because of their prosperity, most carpenters and fishermen were educated.

From the Chinnereth, the Jordan continues to flow south until it empties itself into the Dead Sea which is one thousand ninety-two feet below sea level.

Jesus might be compared to a sea or ocean into which rivers and before them the tributaries have flowed. Jesus seemed to be a collecting basin, the repository of knowledge and spiritual worth. Many were the tributaries that filled his soul. Farmers, fishermen, merchants, sheep herders, all gave to him. For his parables, he used illustrations gleaned from all of them, returning to them the good and the best. The spirit of God, the spirit of love, filled his soul and overflowed onto others.

Moisture from seas and oceans is gathered up into fleecy clouds which, in turn, send showers upon the earth to water the land, flow into streams, brooks, and rivers, and back again to the sea or the ocean. Just as Jesus did, you and I need to gather up the spirit of God, the spirit of love, let it fill our hearts and souls so it will overflow onto all those about us.

GOSSIPING

There are some boys and girls, men and women, who seem to have the knack of saying things in such a way we never forget their words. The Reverend Charles Milluff, minister of a Nazarene Church, is sometimes referred to as the "corncob preacher" because of his ability to take something as simple as a corncob and make it a good teaching illustration. He made a sage observation: "Anyone can count the seeds in an apple, but only God can count the apples in a seed."

There are other boys and girls, men and women, who seem to have the knack of saying things that aren't exactly true but that others enjoy repeating. Gossip is one of the worst things you and I do. On a current television program, a group of girls sing, "We're not the kind to go 'round spreading rumors." Then they pass on what is supposed to be a juicy bit of information regarding a mutual acquaintance.

In this day of ball-point pens there are only a few people who still use fountain pens. Years ago, a manufacturer of fountain pens included a warning with each pen sold, "When the ink flows too easily it may indicate the ink barrel is nearly empty." How many boys and girls do you know who are quite empty-headed but who run off at the mouth?

The word *gossip* in early English was spelled *godsib*. *Sib* meant "related to," so the entire word meant related to God. You know the word *sibling*, which refers to your brother or sister. It was during the time of William Shakespeare that not only the spelling but the meaning of the word began to change. The transition is easy to recognize: When youngsters become close friends—related—they become gossips, talking to each other as siblings.

Jim Larson lives on a farm in Minnesota. One night he was awakened by the barking of a dog. The dog was a long way off, the barking was faint, but it woke Jim and his dog, Nero. Nero responded with his own barking. It wasn't long until a dog living at the farm next to Jim's joined the chorus. Jim lay listening, wondering what it was all about. The dogs didn't know why they were barking either. How many apples can come from a seed?

Bess Robeson, who lived in Redfield, South Dakota, owned a parrot. During the summer Bess would put the bird on the front porch. One day a neighbor's cat got a breeze in its tail and started tearing around like crazy. In the process, it knocked over the parrot stand. The bird was chained to the perch and couldn't fly away, but you should have heard it squawk. It used words that embarrassed Bess. She was glad no one heard the bird for they would have thought she talked in a similar fashion. How many apples can come from a seed?

Someone once wrote: "I move more quickly than the wind. I tear people to bits. I care for no one. Truth means nothing to me, nor does justice. My victims are often innocent, but I don't care. I always remember. I never forget or forgive. My name is rumor."

How many apples can come from a seed? One seed can produce millions of apples.

USE YOUR BRAINS

God gave everyone brains, but some people refuse to use them.

The prophet Ezekiel predicted the fall of Jerusalem. Those who gathered round listened, perhaps nodded their heads in agreement, but paid no attention. The Lord said to Ezekiel, "You are no more to them than a singer of fine songs. They will hear what you have to say but do nothing."

For years, those with understanding have been telling us we have been wasting energy, oil, and gas. But, although folks have listened, perhaps nodded their heads in accord, they haven't heeded the warning; they have continued to waste energy.

Sara Cone Bryant was born in 1873. In 1907 she published a wonderful story about a little boy named Epaminondas. We don't know where Mrs. Bryant found this story; perhaps it had been handed down by word of mouth for generations.

Epaminondas had been visiting his aunt. When he left, she gave him a piece of cake to take to his mother. He clutched it tightly in his hand. By the time he arrived home it was nothing but a fistful of crumbs. His mother admonished him, "You should have wrapped it in some leaves and put it under your hat."

On his next visit his aunt gave him some butter. He carefully wrapped it in leaves and put it under his hat. Of course, when he got home the butter had melted and was running down his face. His mother told him he should have cooled it in the stream first.

The next time his aunt gave him a puppy. When he cooled it in the brook it nearly died. His mother said, "You should have tied a strong string around its neck and carefully led it home."

When Epaminondas' aunt gave him a loaf of freshly baked bread, he tied a string to it and dragged it behind him through the dust of the road.

The boy's mother decided to visit her sister. Before leaving, she baked six beautiful pies and put them on the doorstep to cool. She told her son, "Be careful how you step in those pies!" He was. He stepped in the center of each one.

There is a very old British folk tale which may have been an earlier version of the Epaminondas story. A mother and son lived together. The mother earned their living by spinning, but the son, Jack, did nothing. One day his mother told him that unless he went to work he couldn't eat. Jack got a job with a farmer. Jack was given a penny, but when he got home he discovered he'd lost it. His mother told him he should have put it in his pocket.

The next day the farmer gave Jack a jar of milk. Jack poured the milk into his pocket. His mother said, "You should have carried it on your head."

Next day, soft cheese was his payment. He put it on his head but it melted into his hair. "You should have carried it carefully in your hands!"

A cat was the next day's gift. It scratched Jack as he was carrying it in his hands. His mother said, "You silly boy, you should have tied a string around its neck."

When the farmer gave him a piece of meat the following day, he tied string to it and dragged it home. He was told he should have carried it on his shoulder.

When the farmer gave Jack a donkey, the task of getting it on his shoulders was difficult, but he finally managed.

The author of the book of Hebrews wrote, "We ought to give the more earnest heed to the things which we have heard."

Use your brains!

FROST

Do you like peaches? Some people do; some don't. Some like to eat the fruit but object to the fuzz so must peel their peaches before eating them.

Peaches are grown in many parts of the world. You may even have a peach tree in your back yard. The peaches grown in the state of Georgia in the southern part of the United States of America seem to be special, particularly those from the neighborhood of Cornelia, Georgia. In the center of this city is a statue: a huge red apple, signifying the town to be the Apple Capital of the world as well as the home of delicious peaches. This area may produce such renowned fruit because of the composition of the soil and also the high altitude.

In the spring there is some concern among peach lovers and particularly peach growers about frost hitting after the peach buds have begun to set. If it does, an entire crop may be lost. What is frost? When the atmosphere is chilled just to the point of freezing, water in the air will crystallize on objects. We call this frost. Frost is a usual occurrence in polar regions; in temperate regions mild frosts are also common during cold nights. Sometimes frost may extend over thousands of square miles causing great damage. It isn't the crystals of frost that do the harm; it's the freezing of the juices in the plants or fruit which hurts or kills.

Charles McFee has a good job, a nice home and family. He should be very happy, but he's not. When Charles was six years old he wanted to learn to play a violin. His father agreed and took him to a teacher. The teacher said, "When the boy is eleven or twelve and old enough to learn, bring him back and we'll talk about it. He's too young now."

Charles' ambition was nipped in the bud by a frosty teacher who either didn't know what he was talking about or was too lazy to spend a little extra time with a small child. Yet, history is filled with stories of men and women who have become instrumental virtuosos while still young children. You may have heard of the violinist Yehudi Menuhin who was recognized as a prodigy before he was six. Fortunately, no one froze him in early bud.

When Marty Moore was small, she announced she would like to be a medical doctor when she grew up. Her father said, "Men make better doctors than women." Her mother added, "You'd never catch me going to a woman doctor!" Two freezing blasts of cold right after the other chilled Marty's hopes.

Marty thought her Aunt Margaret would understand so she asked her, "Auntie, I *can* become a doctor, can't I?"

"Yes, sure you can, but don't count on me for any help. You ought to marry and have children."

"But, even if I became a doctor, I still could marry and have children."

Then came the frost that nipped the bud of hope: "Go play with your dolls. Don't talk foolishly."

The writer of the sixty-ninth psalm cried, "Reproach has broken my heart." He might have said, "I continue to get the cold shoulder and it hurts."

Frost can paint beautiful pictures on windowpanes, but the damage it inflicts far outweighs the beauty.

ONE MAN'S MEAT

In many respects the apostle Paul was very opinionated. He spoke his views ardently, with a sense of authority, yet he had the redeeming quality of considering the other person's point of view.

When writing to the people of Corinth, Paul remembered that those who had been brought up worshiping idols did not think as he thought. He suggested that each person does many things that cause others unnecessary discomfort. Those former idolators did things which people in the church didn't like. Paul pointed out, "You upset those former idolaters too." To strengthen his position, he wrote, "If to eat meat offends my brother, I'll not eat meat."

Jim and Isaac play on the same football team. They are friends and could be good friends, but their friendship is shaky because of a characteristic of Jim's which he calls his marvelous sense of humor. He would be shocked if he knew what Isaac calls it.

Jim was born into a Christian home. He has little knowledge of any faith, not even his own. Isaac is an Orthodox Jew and serious about his heritage and beliefs. In the school cafeteria, Jim takes every opportunity to order bacon sandwiches, pork chops, or spare ribs and loudly calls Isaac's attention to the food, knowing that to eat pork is not permitted by Isaac's religion. One evening Jim went out to supper with his parents and was served country ham. Next day he told Isaac, "It was so good even you would have enjoyed it!" Offensive? Yes, and unnecessary.

How much discomfort could be avoided if each of us would remember that the things we like are not necessarily the things our friends enjoy.

Martha Ann smokes. She likes smoking and insists she has every right to smoke anywhere, at any time. However, Christy is allergic to cigarette smoke. It makes her ill. Does Martha Ann have the right she claims?

Because things we say can cause pain, some people will tell you it is never good policy to talk about religion or politics. However, it's not the talking about the religion or politics that does harm; it's the manner of presenting your views that could bring pain. Your thoughts on religion or politics may be very good. If you give them quietly and politely, you may win converts to your way of thinking. Only be careful not to be distressing. Remember Jesus said, "Always treat others as you would like them to treat you."

JET LAG

The town of Oxford, England, is located on the Thames River, but if you look on a map you will be surprised to read the river is called the Isis. That's what the people of Oxfordshire say. Originally, the town was named Oxford because there was a place on the river shallow enough for oxen to cross over. Tc "ford" means to get across a river by wading.

Have you heard your grandparents sing a song about "the old gray mare, she ain't what she used to be"? Dr. George Caird, one of the world's greatest New Testament scholars, was lecturing to a group of North Americans at Mansfield College, one of the colleges which make up Oxford University. He said, "Oxford ain't what she used to be!" speaking in the manner of the song about the gray mare. He continued, "Nothing at the University is the same as it was hundreds of years ago when it began." He mentioned it had started with one college and had grown to forty. He pointed out the many changes in faculty, buildings, and students and concluded, "This has taken a lot of adjustment."

If you fly from Heathrow Airport near London to Logan International in Boston, Massachusetts, you could leave England about noon and arrive in the United States of America about two-thirty in the afternoon of the same day. You might have the same strange reaction that some folk experience. About six o'clock, while those who had not been on a trip were thinking about supper, you would be wanting to go to bed. According to your body time it would be around midnight. The difference in time coupled with the excitement of travel creates a situation referred to as jet lag. It requires some adjusting.

All our lives we must constantly be getting acquainted with something different. We need to make continual readjustments.

Psychologists speak of plateaus of learning. At times we seem to learn rapidly; then for a period we appear to be making no progress whatsoever. This experience is much like jet lag. Changes *are* taking place, things *are* different, but they don't appear to be varied.

When you were a baby you spent some time in a crib with bars at the sides. You wanted to get out and be part of the things happening around you. After a time you may have been placed in a playpen, a bit bigger than the crib. At first it was an adventure, but you soon tired of it and the bars on all sides, and you wanted to be set free.

Finally you were allowed to be on the floor. What a lot of new things to look at and touch. Your life was changed tremendously. For a while you were completely satisfied, but then one room was not enough. You wanted to open the door and go to another room. You couldn't reach the handle though, it was too high. You had to grow some.

It was a great day when you were allowed out into the back yard. This was a splendid happening. There was grass. There were flowers. There were long distances to chase a ball. You fell many times trying to reach the ball. This was like a period of jet lag as you accommodated yourself mentally and emotionally to a new environment.

One day Jesus entered the town of Capernaum which was located on the north end of the Sea of Galilee. He loved the town. He enjoyed the people. The tempo of the community was such that it gave him opportunity to rest. Here he could overcome jet lag and adjust to new situations and problems. One of the disciples asked him, "Who is the greatest in the kingdom of heaven?" Jesus called a little child to him. He answered, "I tell you, unless you *turn round* and become like children, you will never enter the kingdom."

"Turn round" are the significant words. Jesus suggested they should take time to examine their lives, take time to see how they had developed, to see if they

had made the necessary adjustments, or they could not enter the kingdom of heaven.

The eternal something inside of you we call a soul has jet lag sometimes, and you need to take time to let it extend and enlarge and adjust to the new and the different.

HIGH COLORING

Many folk tales come from the far distant past. Most are simple and direct. Folk tales are valuable. They keep alive customs and traditions. They teach history.

Legends, myths, and fables are all part of folk tales. There is a fine line of difference between each of them. Legends are stories built around people who probably did live on earth. Myths are allegories, mystical stories, fictitious narratives, that often involve supernatural people. Fables, also fictitious narratives, usually have animals speaking and acting as humans.

Among the tales of ancient Britain is a well-known story of a chicken out in a garden scratching for worms. A pea falls on her head. She begins to run. A rooster shouts, "Where are you going so quickly, Henny-Penny?"

She replies, "I'm going to tell the king the heavens are falling!"

Cocky-Locky says he'll accompany her. Off the hen and the rooster go, making dust fly until they meet a duck.

"Ducky-Daddles, the sky is falling. We're going to tell the king."

The duck joins the parade. When they meet a goose, he also falls in line.

Along they run until they meet Mr. Fox. When they tell him the sky is falling, he sings out, "Follow me. I'll show you the way to the king." They follow him into his den and that is the end of Henny-Penny, Cocky-Locky, Ducky-Daddles, and Goosy-Poosy.

Mr. Aesop was a Greek slave who was born in the sixth century before the birth of Jesus. He either wrote or gathered together a number of fables and used them in trying to influence people on moral and ethical practices.

He told a tale of a shepherd boy who got bored watching the flock and decided to have fun. He ran back to the village crying, "A wolf is coming. A wolf is coming."

Of course, everyone turned out to help the boy and prevent the wolf from stealing the sheep. The boy began to laugh and admitted he'd only been fooling.

The next time he got bored and ran back crying, "Wolf!" people didn't come out of their homes to help him as quickly as they had on the first occasion and this time they were very angry when they learned he was only playing a game.

It was only a few days later that a wolf actually did attack the flock. The youngster ran screaming to the village, but no one paid any attention.

Fred Sheldon was four years old. One day he ran into his house crying, "There's a lion in the back yard!" When his mother investigated there was nothing in the yard. She told Fred his story was full of high coloring.

When Fred was eight he ran into the house one day crying, "Henry spilled red paint all over the garage!" Henry was Fred's five-year-old brother. Henry was spanked. Later it was discovered Fred was the one who had spilled the red paint. But Henry was the one who suffered.

By the time he was twelve Fred was always saying things like "I ate ten thousand candy bars yesterday."

When he was a senior in high school, Fred bragged, "I just can't understand people who cheat or lie. Why, I've never cheated or lied in my whole life!"

Exaggeration, overstatement, misrepresentation, high coloring—what about it?

STANDING FOR WHAT
IS RIGHT

God has created many beautiful spots on earth. One of these is northern Wales, into which a great deal of loveliness is concentrated into a small area.

On the isle of Anglesey which is part of northern Wales you can visit the town with the longest name in the world. It has fifty-eight letters and is spelled Llanfairpwllgwyngyllgogerychwyrndrobwillllantysil-logogogoch. It is usually called simply Llanfair PG. Translated, the name means "Church, Mary, a hollow, angel, near the rapid whirlpool, Church of St. Marne, cave red."

A wise woman once said the Welsh language is easy if you first swallow a pound of butter to lubricate your tongue before trying to speak. The six hundred thousand folks who speak the language have no problems and need no butter. In Welsh, many words begin with a double *L*. To pronounce them, you place your tongue against your teeth as if you were about to say one *L*, then blow. Out comes a kind of *gl* sound. Be sure no one is in front of you when you try this!

Not far from Llanfair PG is a bridge crossing the

Menai Straits, connecting the island with the mainland near the town of Bangor. Bangor is an interesting small city located in a valley between two mountains. Legend says a man of God came to the spot, built a shelter for himself and a small chapel out of wattle and daub (mud and sticks). Where that chapel once stood there now is a great cathedral where a nice custom is observed once a week. A special candle is lighted and kept burning all day each Thursday to remind people Jesus once prayed that all might be one in his spirit. Folks are asked to pray, not that all people might be the same but that they be united to accomplish much for mankind, that all might stand for the right.

Bangor is in the county of Caernarvonshire, pronounced Carn-are-von-shire. You may have heard that name before because Prince Charles, heir to the British throne, was invested Prince of Wales at Caernarvon Castle. On the road between Bangor and the castle you pass a wall guarding the estate built by Sir Michael Duff, lord high sheriff of the county. It is a beautiful wall, straight, tall, long, giving a feeling of strength and majesty. Suddenly the wall stops, goes back about forty feet, turns to the left and runs along a hundred feet, turns back another forty feet and then again turns right and proceeds in the original straight line.

Why this break in the wall? A house and small garden occupy the indented space. If you inquire, you learn Sir Michael wanted to buy all the land abutting his magnificent home. He ran roughshod, demanding that owners sell to him. Most of the folks were either afraid of him or thought the small sum he offered was a fortune, and sold their property.

However, there was one person who stood firm and said, "No!" She was a lady who had lived in the house all her life. She had been married in that house. She loved her old home. She declared it wasn't right that a great lord should always have his own way. Although the knight threatened, demanded, commanded, ordered, directed, and tried to persuade her, she would not change her mind. She refused to sell. Sir Michael had to tell the workers who were building his wall to detour her property.

That jog in the wall is a monument!